S0-BYQ-421

The Alamo

A Proud Heritage The Hispanic Library

The Alamo

The Fight over Texas

Ann Gaines

Published in the United States of America by The Child's World®
PO Box 326 • Chanhassen, MN 55317-0326 • 800-599-READ • www.childsworld.com

Acknowledgments
   The Creative Spark: Mary Francis-DeMarois, Project Director; Carrie Nichols Cantor, Series
   Editor; Robert Court, Design and Art Direction
   Carmen Blanco, Curriculum Adviser
   The Child's World®: Mary Berendes, Publishing Director

Photos
   Archive Photos: 15; Bettmann/CORBIS: 22, 25, 26; D. Boone/CORBIS: cover; Carrie Nichols
   Cantor: 7; Richard Cummins/CORBIS: 10; George H. H. Huey/CORBIS; Institute of Texan
   Cultures: 8, 18, 19, 30, 32, 33, 35; The State Preservation Board, Austin, Texas: 21, 23; Texas
   State Library and Archives Commission: 28, 34

Library of Congress Cataloging-in-Publication Data
   Gaines, Ann.
     The Alamo : the fight over Texas / by Ann Gaines.
        p. cm. — (A proud heritage series)
   Summary: Describes the history of the famous Alamo, which was built as a
   mission, but later used as a fort, the battle fought there, and its significance
   for the history of the United States.
   Includes bibliographical references and index.
     ISBN 1-56766-173-4 (lib. bdg. : alk. paper)
   1. Alamo (San Antonio, Tex.)—Siege, 1836—Juvenile literature.
   [1. Alamo (San Antonio, Tex.)—Siege, 1836.] I. Title. II. Series: Proud
   heritage (Child's World (Firm))
     F390.G15 2003
     976.4'03—dc21
                                              2002151725

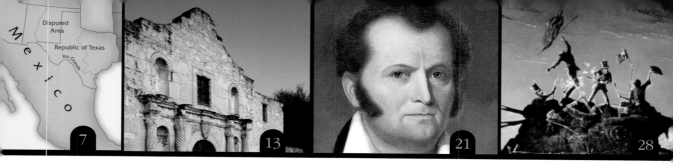

Chapter One

The Alamo Is Founded

The Alamo is a building in the heart of downtown San Antonio, Texas, that has a very special place in American history. It was first a **mission,** next a fort, then a ruin, and now a restored historical site.

Almost 300 years ago, the Spanish built a mission they called San Antonio de Valero in their vast territory in the Americas. The Spanish built hundreds of such missions. This one was much like the others. It didn't become a famous place until years after the mission had closed and its buildings were taken over by soldiers for use as a fort.

A famous battle was fought at this fort in 1836. The Alamo's buildings were largely destroyed in the battle. But the ruins were later restored to serve as a monument. People travel to San Antonio, Texas, from all over the country just to see it and learn more about its history.

The story of the Alamo takes us through some of the most fascinating periods in the history of the Southwest: the Spanish mission era, the Mexican revolution of 1810–1821, the age of America's Western pioneers, and a time of competition between the United States and Mexico for land and power in the Americas. The first

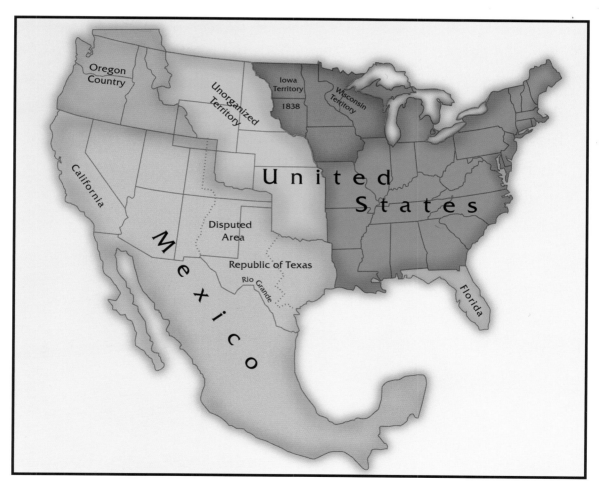

This map shows what the United States and Mexico looked like in 1836, just before the Battle of the Alamo, when Texas was still part of Mexico.

thing to understand is that Texas (as well as Florida, New Mexico, Arizona, and California) was once part of New Spain. It was part of the land called Mexico, which belonged to Spain, just as the 13 American colonies belonged to England.

The Settling of Texas

In 1682, the Spanish built their first settlement in Texas, called Corpus Christi de la Ysleta. Soon they had reason to worry that France might try to take over Texas. So the Spanish began to build more towns, *presidios* (forts), missions, and ranches in the territory. The first were along the Rio Grande. From there, the settlements slowly moved north and east.

The mighty Rio Grande is currently the border between Texas and Mexico.

In the 18th century, when Texas was still part of Mexico and Mexico was part of the Spanish **empire,** San Antonio was an important town. It was the largest Spanish town near the American colonies.

San Antonio's location was so important that the Spanish government ordered five missions to be built there. Its goal was to **convert** the many Native Americans who lived on the nearby plains to Christianity. The missionaries believed that everyone in the world should be Christian. The Spanish hoped that Christian Native Americans would be more peaceful and would not attack the people of San Antonio and other towns.

A mission always included a church and often many other buildings with offices and schoolrooms. The priests and sometimes Native Americans lived at the mission.

Successful missions in Texas usually raised food, including crops and cattle, to feed the converts. Each mission served a different group of Native Americans. Many of the Native Americans were from small tribes that needed protection from larger, more powerful ones.

Some of the Native Americans stayed for only a short time. Others lived at the missions for years. They grew food and raised animals. The priests taught many of these Native Americans to read and write.

Many Native Americans who moved to missions became sick and died. In fact, entire tribes were wiped out by illnesses they got from Europeans. However, many Native Americans found safety in the missions.

San Antonio today is a beautiful, thriving American city.

In 1700, the mission of San Francisco Solano was founded in what is now Mexico, near the right bank of the Rio Grande. It did not do well there. Officials began to talk of moving it. A priest named Antonio de San Buenaventura y Olivares favored a lovely spot farther north with pretty, rolling, fertile land crossed by rivers. At the time, there was nothing there.

In 1716, the Spanish government gave Olivares approval to move the Solano mission to this spot, the future site of the city of San Antonio. On May 1, 1718, a ceremony was held founding the Mission San Antonio de Valero.

A few days later, the governor of the state founded a fort nearby, where Spanish soldiers would live. It was called San Antonio de Béxar Presidio. He also founded a town there called Villa de Béxar. The purpose of the fort was to protect the mission and the town. The government promised to try to find settlers to come live in the town.

Chapter Two

From Mission to Fort

The San Antonio Valero mission had many problems when it was first established. The priests had trouble finding the right place for the mission. At first, it was built a short way from what is today downtown San Antonio, near San Pedro Springs, a good source of water. But it was moved three times over the next few years. After a hurricane destroyed most of its buildings in 1724, the mission moved for the last time, to a spot near the east bank of the San Antonio River. Eventually its buildings would cover 3 acres (1.2 hectares), or more than two large city blocks. Today these three acres are the center of downtown San Antonio.

During the 1730s and 1740s, Native Americans from the northern plains sometimes attacked San Antonio. Comanches—members of a tribe that owned fast horses and many weapons—killed people at the mission, as well as in town and at the fort. In 1739, epidemics of smallpox and measles, diseases brought to the Americas by Europeans, killed many of the Native Americans living at the mission.

But over time the mission became successful. More and more Native Americans came there to live. The missionaries taught some of them how to be weavers, blacksmiths, and carpenters. Others worked in the mission's fields and orchards and on its ranch, where they raised cattle, sheep, goats, horses, and oxen. Still others did construction work.

Buildings That Lasted

In 1727, the priests put mission Native Americans to work building a *convento* for priests, nuns, and missionaries to live in. When the stone building was finished, it stood two stories high. An **arcade** ran in front of the priests' sleeping quarters, kitchens, the dining room, and offices. (Some of this building is still standing today. It is the Long Barracks Museum at the Alamo.)

In 1744, the Native Americans started to build a stone church, but it fell down. A new church was begun during the 1750s. This would be a large and elaborate building. Plans called for it to be built in the shape of a cross, with a dome in the middle and two bell towers. Carvings would cover the front of the building.

The Alamo today is still a very popular tourist site. People travel to San Antonio from all over the country to see it.

By this time, the workers had already built not only the *convento* and homes for themselves but also a building with storerooms and workrooms, a granary, and an *acequia* (a ditch for water). They also built strong walls around the mission to protect against attacks. In 1756, there were 328 Native Americans living at the mission, the most there would ever be.

Missions Are Abandoned

Over the years, four more missions were built in San Antonio. In the 1770s, a new group of missionaries took over management of the Valero mission. But by this time the Spanish government no longer wanted to give much money to missions. The Catholic Church did not have enough money to pay for them all. In 1793, the Spanish government ordered all the missions in San Antonio closed. Their lands, seeds, tools, and animals were all given away. The Native Americans at the missions left.

Some of the San Antonio mission churches were then used for regular church services. But the Valero mission was not. It sat abandoned for ten years.

In 1803, a new company of soldiers was assigned to San Antonio. They used the Valero mission buildings as their living quarters. Spanish soldiers continued to use the Alamo as a fort for the next 18 years.

Americans Flock to Texas

In 1821, Mexico won its independence from Spain after an 11-year war. By this time, many Americans had become interested in the Mexican area known as Texas. Good farmland was becoming scarce in many parts of the eastern United States. More and more people came to his colony.

Stephen F. Austin took over the colony in Texas after his father, Moses, who founded the colony, died.

In 1820, Spain granted an American named Moses Austin the right to start a colony in Texas. The government of the new nation of Mexico said he could go ahead with his plans. When Moses Austin became sick, his son, Stephen F. Austin, took over. Eventually 300 American families came to his colony.

The Mexican government also gave other **empresarios** the right to bring more American settlers to Texas. Thousands of Americans came to Texas during the 1820s. Texas was part of the Mexican state of Coahuila y Tejas.

For a long time the American settlers were content to live in Mexico. But some became dissatisfied with Mexican rule. Some **Tejanos** joined them in talking of independence. Many people wanted Texas to become a new country, no longer part of Mexico. Still others wanted it to become part of the United States.

Fighting over Texas

The United States had already expressed interest in buying Texas from Mexico. But the government of Mexico did not want to lose Texas. It feared that the United States might try to take Texas by force. To prevent this, Mexico sent more soldiers and weapons there.

In 1830, Mexico's congress passed a new law outlawing more Americans from moving to Texas. This angered many of the American settlers who already lived there. There were also other things in the law colonists did not like. The law made slavery illegal in Texas. It also said that Texans would have to pay new taxes. Some Texans wanted Texas to remain part of Mexico but become its own state, no longer joined to Coahuila. This way, they hoped, they would have more say in the government. But the Mexican government would not let Texas separate from Coahuila. During this time, Mexican soldiers continued to use the Alamo as a fort.

Chapter Three

The Texas Revolution Begins

The first battle in what became the Texas Revolution occurred in October 1835. The Mexican government had given the town of Gonzales a cannon to protect it from Native Americans. Now Mexican soldiers were sent to Gonzales to take the cannon back. The settlers would not give it up. A fight took place, and the Texans won. The Mexican soldiers fled from Gonzales back to San Antonio.

When news of this battle spread, other Texans decided they, too, were ready to fight. People from many communities armed themselves and went to San Antonio. They placed the city under **siege.** Over time, more and more people came to help the Texans fight. Some were from the United States.

On December 5, 1835, a Texan named Ben Milam led a charge that started five days of fighting. Milam was killed in the battle. Nevertheless, the Texans won. Mexican general Martin Perfecto de Cós surrendered. The Mexicans retreated, leaving the city—including the Alamo fort—in the hands of the Texans.

No one knew what would happen next. Some people thought there might be peace. But when General Cós returned home and told Mexico's president, Antonio López de Santa Anna, what had happened, Santa Anna was furious. He decided to march to Texas with thousands of soldiers.

When the Texans heard Mexican troops were coming, they tried to prepare. They organized an army and placed Sam Houston in charge. Houston was an American businessman who had

Antonio López de Santa Anna was one of the most colorful figures in Mexican history. He led many battles for the Mexicans, including the Battle of the Alamo, and was president of Mexico three times.

come to Texas to make money. He had experience as a soldier. At that time, although he was known to Stephen F. Austin and other leaders, he was not famous.

The Texans took control of two forts. One was in the town of Goliad. The other was the Alamo in San Antonio. Both were on roads that led from Mexico toward settlements farther east in Texas. The most important responsibility of the soldiers in both places

Sam Houston led the Texans at the Battle of the Alamo. He later became the first president of the Republic of Texas.

was to stand watch. If they saw the Mexican army approaching, they were supposed to send word of its approach to the Texas army. They were also supposed to try to hold the Mexicans there.

Getting Ready for Battle

James Clinton Neill was commander of one of the new Texan army's companies. He and his men were ordered to go to the Alamo. Most of the soldiers with Neill were

Americans who had come from the United States only a few weeks earlier to join the Texan fight. While they were at the Alamo, waiting for something to happen, the soldiers worked on the fort. They strengthened its walls and placed 21 cannons on top of them. They went into town to collect supplies. But there was little there. San Antonio was surrounded by wilderness and not near any other towns.

On January 19, 1836, a new group of soldiers arrived at the Alamo. They were volunteers, not regular members of the army. Their leader was a famous fighter named James Bowie. From the Alamo he wrote to the governor of Texas praising Neill. General Houston had been thinking that maybe the Texans should destroy the Alamo. But Neill and Bowie both believed it was a fort the Texans needed to win the war.

So the Texans agreed to leave the Alamo fort standing. But there was one problem. Neill's men needed horses. If the Mexican army came to San Antonio, they could not send messengers out to warn the settlements farther east. To solve this problem, the army sent even more men to the Alamo.

William Barret Travis and 30 **cavalrymen** arrived at the Alamo on February 3. Five days later, Tennessee congressman Davy Crockett arrived at the Alamo. He was

James Bowie was one of the great heroes of the Texas Revolution. Born in 1796, in Kentucky, he was part of a large family that often moved. As a teenager, Jim Bowie began to earn money by moving lumber down the Mississippi River to market.

As a man, he bought and sold slaves in Texas for a time. Then he and his brother started a business, buying and selling land. In 1830, Bowie returned to Texas. He chose not to settle in Stephen F. Austin's colony but in San Antonio. There he continued buying and selling land.

In Texas, Bowie gained a reputation as a brave and adventurous man. He traveled all over the wilderness, searching for a fabled mine west of San Antonio. He also headed up a ranger troop that fought Native Americans.

When settlers formed an army during the Texas Revolution, Bowie joined as a colonel. He fought in San Antonio in the fall of 1835. In early 1836, he went to the Alamo under orders from Sam Houston. Houston had been thinking of destroying the fortifications there. But Bowie wrote to the government to say he believed this was a mistake. He stayed, only to die along with his men.

William Barret Travis prepared for the arrival of the Mexicans by strengthening the walls of the fort, mounting cannons, and storing supplies wherever he could.

one of hundreds of American men who had decided to join the war. Crockett brought a few more soldiers with him.

On February 14, Neill left the Alamo. He had been granted leave to go home and visit his family. When he left he placed Travis in charge. The volunteers who had come with Bowie did not like this. In the end, Travis took charge of all the regular members of the Texas army. Bowie stayed in command of those who had come in with him.

Davy Crockett was famous long before he went to fight at the Alamo. Born on August 17, 1786, in Tennessee, he was brave and spirited even as a little boy. Stories say he wrestled bears. He first gained fame as an Indian fighter in the Creek Indian War and War of 1812. In 1821, he was elected to the state legislature in Tennessee. He went on to represent the people of Tennessee in the U.S. Congress starting in 1827.

Over the years, he became a legend. People were fascinated by the stories of his exploits as a fighter and hunter. He was even the subject of a series of comic books!

In 1835, Crockett lost his reelection bid and was no longer a member of the U.S. Congress. He was bitterly disappointed. Feeling unappreciated, he decided to go explore the West and headed for Texas.

When he arrived there early in 1836, people were preparing to fight Mexico. Crockett joined in the fight eagerly. He wanted to help Texas first to become independent and then to build its own government. Davy Crockett didn't live to see it happen. He died either at or right after the Battle of Alamo.

The Siege and Battle of the Alamo

The Mexican army had begun to march. It crossed the Rio Grande and headed for San Antonio. The Texans heard it was on its way. For a brief time, at least, Texans who lived farther east knew they would not have to abandon their homes. They organized a meeting at the town of Washington-on-the-Brazos. There men representing settlers throughout Texas decided to declare Texas an independent nation. They wrote the Texas Declaration of Independence.

On February 23, 1836, Mexican president Santa Anna, a general, led 5,000 Mexican soldiers into the city of San Antonio. By that time the soldiers posted at the Alamo had set up for battle inside the fort. Travis wrote a message and sent it to Texans farther east: "The enemy in large force is in sight. We want men and provisions. Send them to us. We have 150 men and are determined to defend the garrison to the last." That very day, a Mexican officer came to offer the Texans a chance to

The Alamo defenders fired their guns at the Mexicans from over the top of the wall of the fort.

Mexican soldiers used ladders to climb up and over the walls of the Alamo.

surrender. In answer they fired a cannonball. Then the Mexicans laid siege to the fort.

The Alamo under Siege

The siege lasted 13 days. On February 24, Jim Bowie became sick. From that point on, he had to stay in bed. These were sad and scary times for the Texan soldiers. Many hoped that others would arrive in time to help them with the battle they knew must come. In the meantime, they fired cannons from the Alamo walls.

Mexican soldiers fired back at them. Santa Anna sent more messages to convince the Texans to surrender. They would not do so.

On March 1, a small group of Texans did cross the Mexican lines to ride into the Alamo. They had come from Gonzales, the nearest town to receive the news that the Alamo was under siege. Historians disagree on the exact number of men who came, but they are remembered as the Immortal 32. They were the only ones who would come to join in the fight.

Finally, tired of waiting for the Texans to surrender, Santa Anna gathered his officers on March 5 to tell them he wanted to assault the fort on the next day. His officers did not want him to do so. They warned him that he had a good chance of winning but that a large number of his soldiers would die in the attempt. He did not back down.

The Assault on the Alamo

On March 6, the Mexican army put Santa Anna's plan into effect. Having awakened in the early hours of the morning, the soldiers lined up. They planned to attack the Alamo from four directions. At around 5 A.M., they marched toward the walls. Warned by lookouts of their approach, the Texans climbed on top of the Alamo's high walls. They took up positions by every cannon.

This painting shows the violence and confusion that must have occurred at the Alamo.

Close to 2,000 soldiers advanced. The 190 men inside the Alamo tried to hold them back with cannon and rifle fire. Many Mexican soldiers fell, and for a moment their advance stopped. But their commanders reformed their lines and drove their men forward to the walls. At close range, they started to shoot Texans one by one. William Barret Travis was one of the first to die. He was shot while he stood on the north wall.

When Mexican soldiers began to scale the walls, the Texans had to fall back. They took up new positions inside the Alamo's rooms. Once the Mexicans were inside, fierce fighting continued. Both sides fired rifles and pistols again and again. Other men fought hand-to-hand. Bowie was shot right in his bed. The chapel fell last.

The Alamo Falls to Mexico

By dawn the battle was over, less than two hours after it had begun. The Texans were defeated. All but seven had died. Those seven were captured, and Santa Anna ordered them shot dead. To this day, historians argue over whether Davy Crockett was one of those seven. By 8 A.M., every Alamo defender lay dead.

That night, under General Santa Anna's orders, Mexican soldiers built a huge **pyre** on which they burned the bodies of the Alamo defenders. Santa Anna had refused to allow the soldiers to be buried. This

How Many Died at the Battle of the Alamo?

An official list of Alamo defenders has 189 names. But some scholars think the number may have been as high as 257. Some say 1,600 Mexicans fell. Others say it was 600.

Here is the Alamo in ruins after the historic battle.

was a sign of disrespect on his part, meant to show other Texans how angry Mexico was.

Mexican soldiers spared the lives of the women and children who were in the Alamo. They were led out of the smoking buildings and offered safety. By that time, Sam Houston had left the convention at Washington-on-the-Brazos, where Texans had declared independence, formed a new government, and written a constitution for their new country. He had joined the Texan army and ordered it to Gonzales. Houston had hoped that the defenders of the Alamo might hold on long enough for the army to come save them.

Now, hearing the news of the terrible defeat, Houston gave orders for all Texans to abandon their homes and flee toward the Louisiana border. This started the Runaway Scrape, during which hundreds of people rode or walked east to keep ahead of the Mexican army.

Nevertheless, despite their great loss, the Texan army continued the struggle. In fact, the battle of the Alamo so angered its soldiers that they were inspired to fight even harder. One group suffered another terrible defeat at the town of Goliad.

The Battle of San Jacinto

The main Texan army met the Mexican army at a small town in Texas named San Jacinto (pronounced san hah-SIN-toe), near Houston, on April 21. Before the battle began, a cry went up, "Remember the Alamo!" Participants remembered that an electric feeling ran through the army. To everyone's surprise, they won the battle. They killed and wounded many Mexican soldiers. They even captured President Santa Anna. Later, participants remembered that they had fought fiercely in part because they were inspired by the Battle of the Alamo.

In this painting, called "The Surrender of Santa Anna," the Mexican president is the person lying down. Part of his left leg appears to be missing. In reality, Santa Anna did not lose his leg until two years later in a battle against the French.

The war ended with the Battle of San Jacinto. In exchange for his freedom, the captured Mexican president Santa Anna agreed to sign a treaty with Texas that said that Mexico would no longer fight with Texas and that granted Texas its independence. However, the Mexican government later refused to recognize Texas as an independent nation.

New Nation

Nevertheless, Texas regarded itself as a new country. Many of the people who had fled Texas during the war returned. They held an election and chose Sam Houston as their new nation's first president. He organized a government.

At that time, most Texans hoped the Lone Star Republic, as it was called, would not exist for very long. They wanted Texas to become part of the United States. There was just one problem. Many Americans did not want Texas to be a part of the United States. Some did not want to bring Texas into the Union because it allowed slavery. Others feared that if Texas became part of the United States, it would lead to war with Mexico.

For ten years, Texas remained an independent nation. Thousands of immigrants poured into Texas. The new country grew rapidly.

TEXAS!!

Emigrants who are desirious of assisting Texas at this important crisis of her affairs may have a free passage and equipments, by applying at the **NEW-YORK and PHILADELPHIA HOTEL,** on the Old Levee, near the Blue Stores.

Now is the time to ensure a fortune in Land: To all who remain in Texas during the War will be allowed 1280 Acres.
To all who remain Six Months, 640 Acres.
To all who remain Three Months, 320 Acres.
And as Colonists, 4600 Acres for a family and 1470 Acres for a Single Man.

New Orleans, April 23d, 1836.

This advertisement was published in New Orleans in April 1836. Its purpose was to get people to come to Texas during the war with Mexico.

This drawing depicts Texas's president Anson Jones lowering the flag of the Republic of Texas when Texas became part of the United States.

Finally, in 1843, James K. Polk became president of the United States. He was the first president who wanted to make Texas part of the United States. During his administration, the United States invited Texas to become a state. The people of Texas voted in favor of becoming part of the United States. On December 29, 1845, Texas became the 28th state in the United States, and the Lone Star Republic existed no more.

Honor for the Alamo

In the years after the Texas Revolution, the Battle of the Alamo became a legend. Historians wrote long, detailed accounts of the battle. It became the subject of songs and poems.

For a long time, the fort remained in ruins, but it was recognized as an important historic site. Interest in its preservation grew. An organization called the Daughters of the Republic of Texas bought and restored the property. Today thousands of tourists visit the Alamo every year to learn about its roles as both mission and fort.

This 1893 photo shows a celebration in front of the Alamo commemorating the battle that had taken place almost sixty years earlier.

The moral of the story of the Alamo is that sometimes there is victory even in defeat. The defenders of the Alamo were all killed, but their courage inspired others to fight on and win. They are still remembered and honored generations later.

1492: Christopher Columbus reaches the Americas.

1521: Spain conquers Mexico.

1682: The Spanish build their first settlement in Texas, Corpus Christi de la Ysleta.

1700: The mission of San Francisco Solano is founded in what is now Mexico, near the right bank of the Rio Grande.

1709: A priest named Antonio de San Buenaventura y Olivares travels in to what is now Texas to look for new places to build missions. He especially likes the future site of San Antonio.

1716: The Spanish government gives Olivares approval to move the Solano mission to San Antonio.

1718: In May, a formal ceremony is held marking the beginning of the Mission San Antonio de Valero.

1724: The Valero mission moves for the third and last time, to a spot near the east bank of the San Antonio River.

1727: The priests in charge of the Valero mission set the mission's Native Americans to work building a *convento,* a stone building with offices, workrooms, and bedrooms for them.

1739: Epidemics of smallpox and measles, diseases brought to the Americas by Europeans, kill many of the Native Americans at the Valero mission.

1744: The Native Americans start to build a stone church for the Valero mission. After it falls, they start work on a second, which still stands today.

1756: The San Antonio Valero mission's population reaches its highest number ever, with 328 Native Americans living there.

1793: Because of their expense, the Spanish government orders all the missions in San Antonio closed, including the Valero mission.

1803: Spanish soldiers begin using the Valero mission buildings as a fort. From this point on, the mission is called the Alamo.

1821: Mexico wins its independence from Spain. Americans begin moving to Texas in large numbers.

1835: The Texas Revolution begins. After a small group of Texans win the Battle of Gonzales, a larger army is formed. It forces the Mexican soldiers stationed in San Antonio to leave Texas.

1836: Texan soldiers move into the Alamo and prepare to defend it. On February 23, 1836, Mexican general Antonio Lopez de Santa Anna leads 5,000 Mexican soldiers into the city of San Antonio and lays siege to the Alamo. On March 6, the Texans lose the Battle of the Alamo. On April 21, they win the Battle of San Jacinto. Texas becomes an independent country, the Lone Star Republic.

1845: Texas becomes the 28th state in the United States.

arcade (ahr-KAYD) An arcade is a covered passageway that runs along the side of a building. Many arcades have arches. An arcade ran along the Alamo's main building, the convento.

cavalrymen (KAH-vuhl-ree-men) The cavalry is the branch of an army that is trained to fight on horseback. William Barret Travis led a group of cavalrymen at the Alamo.

convert (kun-VERT) To convert means to convince a person to change from one religion to another. Missionaries in Texas wanted to convert Native Americans to Christianity.

empire (EHM-pire) An empire is a country that conquers and rules over other countries or colonies. Britain, Spain, and France all had large empires that included lands in the Americas.

empresarios (em-pruh-SAH-ree-ohz) Empresarios were people given land in Texas by the government in exchange for starting a colony there and bringing in settlers. Stephen F. Austin and Green DeWitt were both empresarios.

mission (MIH-shuhn) A mission is a religious community built by missionary priests who want to spread their religion. Native Americans came to Texas missions to live, learn, and worship.

pyre (PIRE) A pyre is a pile of wood for burning dead bodies on. The Alamo defenders' bodies were burned on a pyre.

siege (SEEJ) Soldiers lay siege when they surround a fort or town to try to get it to surrender. Mexican soldiers laid siege to the Alamo starting on February 23, 1836, trapping Texans inside for 13 days.

Tejanos (teh-HAH-noze) The Mexicans living in Texas before the Revolution called themselves Tejanos. The Spanish word for "Texas" is *Tejas,* and for "Texans" is *Tejanos.* Many Tejanos joined the American settlers and fought for independence from Mexico.

Further Information

Books

Burgan, Michael. *The Alamo*. Minneapolis: Compass Point Books, 2001.

Santella, Andrew. *The Battle of the Alamo*. Danbury, Conn.: Children's Press, 1997.

Stanush, Barbara Evans. *Texans: A Story of Texan Cultures for Young People*. San Antonio, Tex.: Institute of Texan Cultures, 1988.

Web Sites

Visit our Web page for lots of links about The Alamo:
http://www.childsworld.com/links.html

Note to parents, teachers, and librarians: We routinely monitor our Web links to make sure they're safe, active sites.

Sources Used by Author

Groneman, Bill. *Eyewitness to the Alamo*. Houston, Tex.: Republic of Texas Press, 1996.

Hardin, Stephen L. *Texian Iliad: A Military History of the Texas Revolution*. Austin, Tex.: University of Texas Press, 1994.

Jenkins, John H., editor. *The Papers of the Texas Revolution, 1835–1836*. 10 volumes. Austin, Tex: Presidial Press, 1973.

Lord, Walter. *A Time to Stand*. New York: Harper, 1961; 2nd edition, Lincoln: University of Nebraska Press, 1978.

McComb, David. *Texas: An Illustrated History*. New York: Oxford University Press, 1995.

Simmons, Helen, and Cathryn Hoyt, editors. *Hispanic Texas*. Austin, Tex.: University of Texas Press, 1992.

The New Handbook of Texas. 6 volumes. Austin, Tex.: Texas State Historical Association, 1995.

Index